For Girls
(& Others)

For Girls
(& Others)

SHANNA COMPTON

BLOOF BOOKS

Published by Bloof Books
www.bloofbooks.com

Bloof Books are distributed to the trade via Ingram, Baker & Taylor, and other wholesalers. Individuals may purchase them direct from our website, from online retailers such as Amazon.com, or request them from their favorite bookstores. (Please support your local independent bookseller whenever possible.)

ISBN: 978-0-6151-6697-1

For Girls

Comedy of Manners

For Girls

PREFACE.

THE author of this book lays no claim to originality of subject-matter. She has nothing new to say. She does, however, claim originality upon one ground, that of making selections from the writings and teachings of others, and from observation and experience; that of culling here and there knowledge, facts, motives, ideas, and grouping them into practical form.

Seeking to make the material for instruction as complete as possible, she has seized upon and appropriated anything which could contribute to the general design. She has only sought to adapt what others have said to the good of the class for whom she has written.

She herewith submits her efforts to the common sense of her audience, and the common need of our common natures.

Opening Address

We shall now begin
the study of girls
upon whom the universe
bestows fullness
in all the right places.

A vigorous strength
can belong to a real lady
& her natural waist.
Young men ought to be taught
to appreciate her unbound form
& exquisite mental
susceptibility.

There is much to say
upon the body & mind
of young woman
& so I present you
47 chapters to follow
after this gentle foreword.
I will endeavor to illustrate
more delicate matters
in a manner suitable for
even the most innocent.

Here it befalls us to wonder
upon this first astonishment:
A girlhood is an extreme gift
of boobies & hips
of blossom lips &
the good sense
not to use any of them.

The Young Lady Must

Grow your frilliest beauty
on your dearest fanny

Blow your daintiest trumpet
on your weariest wonder

& never ever let them
see you perspire

•

Furthermore

if life has not yet
made you its own trusted confidante,
take heart

The world is like a girl
who rivals you in grace
& good looks

Go cautious
in your motions & she
will come around to call you friend

The Head Needs Rather to Be Kept Cool

Situate yourself
alone for longer
than an hour apart
without speaking

The air wants words in it

The house around
adrift, surrounds
surges close

In front of the millinery
the street is spread
with late spring snow,
bristles with girls in hats

Unfold this shuttered voice

& when solitude's good pupil
chooses unfrivolous company
endeavor to
             bare it

No Slight Affliction, as Many a Woman Will Declare

You can carry, girls,
a little distance

your influence
to the new side

your awakened study
of formation, requirements

•

First then, girls, you should
fasten onto your shoulders

a strap for purpose,
for industrious earnest

pressure, for attending
to the demands of nature

Think of it
as a uniform

outside of which
you'd be too apart

•

All rooms have doors
& also windows

I haven't actually
heard that said, but

a draft *might* come
at right angles

toward the animal
part of you,

the portion you've
bitten raw

Pride in Having Small Feet

Overstrung
ailing
puny
inefficient
unhappy
slimsy girls
bustled & padded

With such carriages as these
equipoise is nearly impossible

•

Mental beauties
open yourselves
    o   pen

Being "all used up"
every day for weeks is wrong

& doubles
the myriad feminine dangers
of nervous force

•

I, too,
without a word of excuse
formerly lived as an unmitigated ninny

Linger upon the chaise
of this simple lesson:

Might you unlearn
to resent the joy
the world takes in you,

learn
to return its gaze

On Thinking for Oneself

The author recommends it,
& tenders her readers
beneficent assistance by thus
beginning & concluding
this book's briefest chapter

Besides the Dress

So this is your minimalist
dressing table

Your soundless powder

Brushes hushed
in a cracked glass

A dust

A hair listlessly

•

Don't bother
to call him sir

It makes him feel old

A swipe or two toward the eyes
A strap adjusted
Lift & plump, tease
spritz

A buckle
A hook like a tooth

•

Daily
& most nights

how many
of you
sit in this chair

pouting at each other

crowding round your face
to see

which of you
you will choose

to clothe

to walk out

Some May Demur

Corsaged, the sweep of hair
back from your brow

& row upon row
of unfumbled buttons

A rescued grimness
perches on your three-quarters face

Overpreened plumage

of bouffant sleeves
& pintucked pleats

The air in the room
                        suspends

a drift of talcum

When the century mounts
will you complete your turn

to face it

To Lessen the Sum of Human Woe

One may be
the best
a girl may

being an open self
permeable

marriageable at will
unto another
becoming

accustomed to
the hair along his thigh

she must
just as he must

the peculiarities
of woman's thinking

on passion
as a subordinate
power

to the primate
nature

sluicing ever
as water

over its stones

The Wise Girl Will Prepare Herself as Well as She Can to Be Happy

You are a bird
inside this cage

Sing

Throw your body
into the air

Urges in Regard to Which Girls Should Receive Especial Instruction

Regretfully I cannot let
another chapter pass
without mention
of the secret bad habits

I will be as plain as I may

Touching
fingering
handling &
playing

in a manner not necessary
for cleanliness

rob the complexion
of rosy blood
by calling it down
toward lustier cheeks

When you notice girls
going about dead pale
with dark purplish rings
what other matter
can be blamed?

Admittedly
there are some girls
who claim to do it
long & often
without falling ill

But take my word:
such a female is in reality
tormented almost unto madness
by spells, deliriums
& spasms

Our Mission to the Race

When you're a girl
the moon belongs

There's a song

It shows its hooks & eyes
It trembles its single number

It is rather stupid, but sweet
It steps like a barefooted boy
It never stops growling

Upon your health
recuperative
its charm

You must be loose
with it, the moon

Taunt it twenty different ways
in as many days
to tax its nature

Let us see
what can be done
with a mere bald planet

Subjects of Private Interest

The very verb
obtain

taken but with
little empathy

A rumpled promise
to a rumpled suitor

A tempt
to woo

A toe
a shoe

An arm
a lacy garment

A calf
a laugh

& to be emphatic:
never hairy!

A Special Physiology

Say, for sake of argument
that to lighten her cares
a girl ceases altogether
to be fickle

She will stop
working too hard

She will settle her heart
into the cradle
of someone else's
& not be aimless or scant

All dear girls linger
upon this point

At first

•

A girl loses
many particles over time
like any article
that can become worn out

She teases eventually
every unfrayed fiber
by use of it

On the other hand,
if she were never
to employ herself
to any end at all

her body would hang
around herself
as the sleeve hangs
on an underdeveloped arm

An ideal girl
learns or intuits
her elastic pattern
of use & ease

She will end as
she never knew she began

the daughter
of no mother but herself

Mistake for Modesty

Docility, the gentle
positioning of

oneself along the edge
of oneself

anticipating the spilling
over into a wellful

•

Make a graceful arc
as you enter
your splash

Inhabit the skipped stone
Exercise the ripple

Otherwise mingle

The Fitness of the Soul

These figures
ought alone to think

further upon basic
wickedness

of which complaint
has been made

& then discarded

•

The sensibility re: right conduct

once cut off
from circulation

shrivels until it is merely
five or six inches long

What Enfeebles the One Enfeebles the Other

Ailing, confined,
curtailed

she wastes
good talents

malingering in a bed
developing chronically

•

She might well
have become cynical

or utterly slack
She bullied herself

to save others
the chore

•

Her chief enthusiasm
each nurse's surprise

that she breathed,
sang, shifted herself about,

looped line
after flyaway line

To Appear Out of Season

She gives

Her likeness mirrored

for a pleasantry
a vision

From hours of toil
at a piano

tumbles slight music
on a happenstance afternoon

As rain
As rain

Antiqued prepositions

A grammatical flourish,
the curl lying against her neck

Hers
this interior
furnished

All's paramour
greening
in her selfy muck

Which buds
bear

the grace of hands, practiced
seeming unpracticed

Run wild a weed
among accidental
ornamentals

In the corner
an orchid droops
from inadequate misting

Shoots so pale & rare

even a gardener grown up in the trade
may not know them

She plucks
herself

A Blemish of Temper

We look over
a woman's station
to determine
at what point to

take just such a yoke
& make it roomy
enough

•

Don't, girls
Don't say that

Broken in upon
by the demands
of first this

looking desirable
rough, saucy, lazy,
heedless, untidy, impolite,
mischievous
(a perennial favorite)

the more intimate,
the more excellent
outward applications

•

Let the muslin out

Oh your shoulders, girls
& under them
after a distance, where
if you please

great harm &
a considerable draft
withdrawn

fill the lungs
with fresh air
even to the minutest cell

•

Modes will doubtless
continue to change
& may far exceed
the pleasures
of contemporary girlhood

We aim for the good sense
that cannot be awakened
in just any girl

We continue to prepare
our simple book

Comedy of Manners

The Debutante

There she is
arranged for public
inspection

She's gratefully refused
stuffed whittled curled
poofed painted encased
enlarged enhanced plucked
tightened covered colored-in
& denied knowing anything about

Her so-called sacrifices
have been considerable,
a punishment with which
she titillates herself

Oh fantasy reward!

But the grand permission
she sought has turned out
to be a rather tepid
approval

& the expectation
that she keep it up
practically forever

Pruning of the Shrubby

Think of growing the funny little things
in your own garden from seed
Find & love an unpretentious patch

A pinkish variety is known
as the maiden's blush

If your aim is ornamental,
ostentatious but without poison,
she may be slipped
until she is tall & decorative

Likewise a gift of old growth
in water or sand
she may be coaxed to give off
the heady scent of roses

A balm with hairy leaves
Yellow, variegated
Nutmeg or apple-scented
Large, dark green, velvety
A true fingerbowl geranium

Her feathery foliage
spreads rapidly

She is very white & woolly

Better known as sweet asylum

The Bloody Intellect

What has she done
with her white feathered dressing gown
her getaway rococo as dream?

Misplaced her tongue
along a redundant ear
in error, in sorrow, with intent.

Beginning with white
is to erase the body,
blank the self
to receive the costumes it consumes.

Potted plants stand in trios,
pointed & pruned. Trained
with snipping & ties.

So public a face, hers,
it hardly belongs.
A camera. All poses. All lies.

If No New Continent or Ice Barrier Intervene

A married woman seems to be
her own improvidence
or impulsive generosity.

The married woman still retains
the use of her real
(as her husband has of his)
disposing of either
she may sock away the profits, i.e.
the impregnable fortress of Realism.

Secured to her shall be the homestead,
herself, and her minor comfortable home,
plus the subjectivity of honor and desire—
after the man's disease is ridden out.

Still better than these ameliorations
of tartly woeful rigors,
the exigencies of social life
do require a general disposition
to yield a careful patient
in appealing need of doctoring.

She might take in
all mind with matter
and make a vast (yet dainty) stride towards
profoundly discriminating truths
and a heroic career of discouragement and peril,
where the Advance lays frozen in Greenland.

Let her assemble
(wrapped in silken robes and tied with a perky ribbon)
an entirely fresh narrative
full of interest and possessing that peculiar fascination
which so naturally attaches
to stories of personal adventure
amid the wild and unique desolations.

The Offices of Women

Think of her
as kindling

informed by light
such

that it collects
at her bright tips

Come under
the power of

her example:
the necessity of abandon

a theme of memory
& spiritual comeliness

a blandishment
to which none can hold

all ladies

Young America, in a Dress Coat at Seventeen, Finds Them All to Be Monstrous Slow

Having neither a remarkably fine figure
nor a Paris gown

nor a distinguishing talent
for piquant conversation (in public)

she nevertheless has had ample leisure
to observe her sometime suitor's

devotions to shallow,
overdaubed, underdressed women

& scorns the cheap stimulus
as chief social pleasure

develops a little sourer,
an active, intense individuality

•

Names spoken lightly in evening,
the prolonged enchained attentions of a man

—the attentions which women would not be women
if they did not like to receive—

all the goings and comings
of Summer days by the sea,

fall to the class of
frivolity & flirtation

●

Poor censure.
Perhaps she should write a pamphlet.

●

Becoming more and more extravagant
in her dress & habits

she is forced to surround her person & home
with the sensuous attractions

by which the demimonde
allures loose husbands away

She might go further,
might be less lavish in outlay
& more modest in dress

if she were led to suppose
that men liked it better

A Novel

A woman & a man.
A woman in a dress.
A gesture of announcing.
A man giving a speech.
A woman looking shocked.
A woman looking displeased.
A man & woman looking downward.

•

Ladies sitting at a table talking.
Ladies drinking tea.
A lady fanning herself.
A woman pointing to the left.

•

A graceful speaker.
A gesture of declaring.
A gesture of meditation.
A gesture of awe or appeal.
A gesture of silence.
A man putting on his glove.
A man with his hat on.
A man at a door.
A man with a suitcase running to catch a train.

•

A woman & her dog at a cupboard.
A woman with food.
A gesture of wonderment.
A gesture of resignation.
A flash of anger.

•

A man in a tuxedo boasting.
A man expressing joy with his hands clasped.
A gesture of annoyance.
A gesture of repulsion.
A man expressing malice with clenched fists.
A man with tall boots shooting a gun into the air.
A man looking shocked.
A dandy man slouched in his chair.

•

Ladies drinking tea.
Ladies strolling through a park.
A woman alone in a small house.

•

A man sitting at a writing desk.
A man reaching to pick something up.
A gesture of remorse.
A man wrapping two small boxes in paper.

•

A woman sitting in a chair.
A woman looking at a piece of paper.
A gesture of repulsion.
Her features softening.
A gesture of remorse.

•

A man at a door.
A woman standing with a bowl of flowers.
An awkward speaker.
A gesture of presentation.

A gesture of refusal.
A gesture of offering.
A gesture of receiving.
A gesture of acceptance.
Their gestures of gladness.

This is a curious machine.

I am something like
its switch.

Her great-grandmother asked the family "to dress" before entering the living
room where the television waited.

A page of equations
Looking at a spread
of characters feeling
nothing/something

She left a long note
in cursive
listing everything
she took

What I need is a map
to circumvent this mood

Addressed it
to herself & dropped it
unstamped
no less certain

*All conversation except the Essential was permitted. Though a plate was fixed for
him on each occasion, no one spoke to or of the Problem Uncle. He persisted (& the
others too) until at last he died.*

Begins with *F*, Ends with *Uture*

Poise is important
in a situation like this.
Macho traffic noise
might muffle us
to distraction but today
we're getting a glimpse
of spring green
enough to welter
a full year.

I'm comforted
by my own usefulness
like a domestic object.
I hope I bloom soon,
petal out to peal
with sentences full
of sniffles.

I feel like a building super
stymied by middling weather.

Dear Bread & Butter,

We had such a lovely
immensely meeting yr
company of wonderful swimming
& sunshine overnight.
What a charming handwritten
engagement informally appropriate
with good friends.

The wife,
as social secretary,
usually writes.

The Dome Is It

The opposite of *no* within
the curved, complete shape
of your dreamed conveyance.
Everything you've said lately
so similar to immediate
but not quite so. The skin
of early spring is bared before
your mouth, a glossy slice
of something new.
When later comes
everything you've said's
just left your lips
and manages to stay true.
This is the way we pass
several days, without work,
without anything but speaking
and reading lines aloud.
If you thought of a number
I would know it, and it would
be whole and even, next to
nothing, but just the right amount
of time or anything it measured.
Running alongside us
goes everybody else.
The balance is good.

Whence All This Delight?

At the usual manner
in the usual hour
a huge, hideous
buck invigorates
the general monotony

Halloo the mutant thing

Our boys
instantly to their guns
till

It raises a whoop
emits a hearty
roused resolution
of animal bleating
the like of which
no two small girls
who had been a little absent
could assimilate

These things happen

Our boys
instantly to their guns
till

Headless Female Torso

In violet light
she rises
to a tart
peach drapery.

Cashes in
the sleepy hours
for something readier
in quicker gold.

She fills out
another set of cards.

She scans the blue
books along the shelf
& chooses a thick one.

Opens it
anywhere
to find the subtle
bubbles of her thoughts
bursting with noiseless pops
& a little spittle.

First, we'll drown.
Then the ice will come.

Endless sheets
of white ice
reaching to cover her
consoling roundness.

Romance

Admit you don't love aimless June,
the midsummer month, too hot to stress
& sweat & fidget beneath the moon.
The bullfrog's oboe tones obsess
the reeds, throaty come-ons for copper snakes.
Well, that's pretty nice. Perhaps the month is moot.
& there's the namesake bug, its anticake-
walk leavings, chairs for former marchers, beaut-
iful jewels clipped to the screens, as if bedecking Garbo's
swanny neck, the dramatic arc of a sultry drive-in play.
She could save all summer. She could kiss the hobo,
then he'd go on to earn it, to get a designer day
job tying hankies to sticks. They'd lie under rhinestone
skies off the tracks to Texas. She'd learn to love his rank cologne.

The Blue One with the Tail

Tentatively & brave
to be examined
she's standing
over to the left

She's done this
so many times but

her recollection's
scratched out
or sort of faded

It's just kind of floating there

She's painted her toenails
& framed them
in a strappy sandal
with a tall stacked heel

What type of animal
has a tail with stripes
like that?

She's reached out
but never touched it

Terminal

Wilma trails her beefy fingers
along the counter,
adoring the formica.

She's positively flocked
with peach fuzz, a pale
auburn fizz atop her skin.

Dark Carla relights the pilot,
reaches toward his gashole
with a fireplace match.

Carla's cleavage is frocked
in polyester and reeks
of roses & Lemon Joy.

The joint's the cook con's fool cure
to ward against recidivism,
The Run Way. He busted out in '92.

A plump king among fools,
the pilot's indiscriminate, gorged
on the diner grub, scored

and glazed by a couple of bored
broads sporting nametags.
In twenty he takes to the sky.

Carla & Wilma cave and have pie.

The More Lenient Personals

Soft
pink
& forlorn
is how we like them best

No trouble
to clutch

Only a few little irritants
& those should be
marginally adorable

Dependability
is good
like a bonus of 3 extra ozs.
in a bottle of shampoo

(There's always more where)

Sure, a fellow can dream
of magnetic, fluid, beastly, cursive, yelpmouthed, heckling, unfolded,
accelerated, improbable, opaque, wayward, damp, grieving willingnesses
who are all forgiveness

so go ahead & call

It comes with its feet
already shaped like that

Powersuit

The lift major
a choppy gel do
brash the palette
in knifelike swipes
the wedge the fingers make
spackled against the cheek

Collar triangular
a waist in-nipped
by patent's lurid gloss
a peplum angled to mimic
blocky shoulders' splay

Menswear print
of houndstooth bitten
or solid bold assured
squared the buttons
four overlarge matured

A skirt severe geometry
a nylon sheath's control
a vamp surreal
a spiked tall heel
a bluntly pointed toe

Incantatory
morning glory
a conjuring
a drag

The Blonde Stigma

Gummy figures
as if from bad paintings
enact historically
under the lights
of the parking lot

Apparently it's cheaper
not to fake the effects

A girlish blob to the right
lowers a hand
looks about to stand
wishes hard
rushing the end

The Groggy Parade

In her farthest mind
a summer

In her nearest
something white
in flake form

After a while
a place gets crowded
& begins to feel like a body
under revision by a virus

She's goofy on cold&flu
dreaming of
      hallways
      smokestacks
      cartoon monsters

Rows of windows
studded with cooling units

A fringe of trees

We're loving it.

A blue photograph
of course contains sky.

It was taken from a car window.
A push upward during a movement forward.
Stripes flicking through the asphalt sling.

Night arcs add to a continuous sense
of April, this year. Please welcome.

To the pink pages, thank you.
Thank you parasol. Thank you fuzzy voiced
at the mike. Thank you ice in a glass.

The road is a method, or a line joining
one possible former with a likely latter,
like a ladder.

And yes, the sky is blue.
And it can be photographed.

Our official position is class piñata.
Our innermost breaks.

Awful White Wine

I am a head & a half
taller than our city's police commissioner.
A head that hurts & is gorgeous noxious.

The gown of evening sequins
like stepdancers between
the two bridges & bagpipes my double-v dress.

The baby in the Swee'Pea outfit
poses for photographs along the long bare arms
of the younger girls & with most of the ruddier pops.

All night the cervix of Our Lord
glistens & slurps with an enlarged pink
fiddling sound. We're ready to ascend.

Here's What She Should Do

What she should really do
after her long day of filming is done
is talk to her doctor or school nurse.
What she should do is stop and wait while I take a leak.
What she should do: Get with the times.
You ppl are getting so freaking off topic.

She recognizes that if she knew only the facts—
that Dad picked me up and squirted something wet on my neck—
she'd have a lot less trouble at the office.
She won't admit it, but she loves to feel the impact.

What she should do is clarify her position:
She likes it when I decide to do things my way.
She likes it when we're following her, behind her.
She likes it when Colonial Williamsburg conducts
a Cry Witch program at the courthouse.

She likes it when I rub her brownish fur.
You'll see how she likes it.

If possible, give her a goal and let her
go to school and make something of her life.
What she should really do is stop going to the gym,
put the mayo back on her bread, and enjoy this time.

Won't Stick to Wounds

She seems to want to recast
her slutty, flighty, rich-bitch, bimbo image

Foofaraw deal-with-it rants
for gentle removal
losing only a little hair

It's always a good time
to adjourn

Actually, all of them are adopted
& she's sure someone else
signed the papers

in a short session,
as if there were no provisions
to see her through

We Know She Knows about Her Elephantine Legs

I can understand trousers are comfortable
but she's a woman.
She should ditch the blobby trousers
to hide her fat veiny legs
& make it easier to find her penis.

She should ditch the Botox
She should ditch that Puritan look
She should ditch the dude and BE IN SCHOOL
She should ditch her third husband fast
ditch her asshole father
ditch her overgrown lips
ditch her personal relationship with Jesus
ditch her Mimi-like makeup & booze
ditch her overzealous manager & production team
She should ditch the creep who knocked her up
& try dating someone who's actually into her.
She looks like a big black garbage bag filled too full.

But she did the skirt and dress thing.
Now it's time to put on the big girl pants
and kick some ass.
How about a bag over her face and a gag in her mouth?
She should A) lay off the tanning beds,
B) stop dressing like a Vegas call girl,
C) give up on the white lipsticks,
and finally D) dig up some sturdy, thick man legs
supporting a desperate piercing sound.
How appealing.

She needs a big helping
of shut-the-fuck-up
and an extra dose of shawl or small detailing
so she can look as smart as she is.
If she'd just try a little EXERCISE.

The American People just want
to tap that feminine side
(except the cankles)
all the way to the White House.

Addressing the Fact That I Am a Bad Person

I have failed you.
I just had chocolate cake for breakfast.
I have more sweaters than any one person really needs.
I do not have links up.
My socks are not sufficiently minimalist.

I am a bad person, blahblahblah.

My boyfriend doesn't know how
to communicate with me in native language.
He's seen medications of mine.
I've never had an orgasm with him.
I'm angry that he chooses video games
over spending time with me.

My boyfriend doesn't know any of this.

This is about me trying to understand
why all of this is happening.

My father always kids around saying I'm fat.
My whole family doesn't know what to say.
My family doesn't know I blog.
My entire family doesn't know the meaning of the word.
What if my family doesn't know what conditions are in the family?

I don't like having to explain things away.

Here I was, going through life,
enjoying the pleasures of psychedelics.
On the internet, nobody knows you're a dog.
Nobody knows it's coming along nicely.
Nobody knows but Jesus.

I don't really want to tell my mom about this stuff.
She will freak out.

At least my mom thinks I'm cool.
She thinks I'm rad.
But my mom thinks I'm handsome, 27 years old, male.
Yes, even my mom thinks I'm a shithead.
She thinks I made it all up.
She said puppies will roam.

Well, I think I am a bad person almost all waking hours.
I blame everything wrong happening around on me.
I'm about to do something wrong
with forethought, although no malice.

How can you resist a kitten?

Notes

For Girls

"Preface" is lifted verbatim from *For Girls: A Special Physiology,* by Mrs. E. R. Shepherd, an popular health manual for girls and young women first published in 1882 by Fowler & Wells and reprinted through the 1890s in more than twenty subsequent editions.

Though they are not found poems, most of the rest of the pieces in this section borrow their titles or other phrases from the same book, heavily remixed and freely recontextualized.

Comedy of Manners

The poems in this section also frequently beg, borrow, or steal from sources ranging the 19th, 20th, and 21st centuries, including gardening manuals, adventure periodicals, sermons, etiquette books, religiously inflected medical texts, promotional pamphlets for household products, a clip art catalog, art criticism, newspapers, and the Internet.

The Blue One with the Tail: This poem is inspired by an untitled painting by Elizabeth Zechel. Some of Elizabeth's work can be found online at clunkytown.blogspot.com.

We Know She Knows about Her Elephantine Legs: "I can understand (trousers) are comfortable but she's a woman and she is allowed to show that," remarked Italian fashion designer Donatella Versace in *Die Zeit,* February 8, 2007, speaking of presidential candidate Senator Hillary Rodham Clinton and her infamous pantsuits. The poem mines comment-stream responses to this so-called news as they appeared on the *Huffington Post* website, mixing them with similarly phrased "she should ditch" advice for women supplied by an Internet search engine.

Acknowledgments

Much love and many thanks to my friends, first readers, and this book's editors, who I'm pleased to say are all the same bunch: Tom Beckett, Anne Boyer, Jennifer L. Knox, Ada Limón, Danielle Pafunda, Maureen Thorson, and my husband Shawn Hollyfield.

Thanks also to Mom, who turned me on to the work of Mrs. E. R. Shepherd; to Ian Keenan, who made me a gift of several other useful books; to Elizabeth Zechel, whose painting inspired the poem "The Blue One with the Tail;" to CAConrad, Joshua Corey, David Lehman, Reb Livingston, Charlie Orr, Ron Silliman, Gary Sullivan, and the members of Pussipo and the Flarflist.

My gratitude to the editors of the following publications, in which some of these poems first appeared:

Absent: "The Groggy Parade"

Court Green: "Romance"

Dusie: "We're loving it.", "The Bloody Intellect," and "A Novel" appeared in issue 5. "The Debutante," "Pruning of the Shrubby," "The Blue One with the Tail," "The More Lenient Personals," "Headless Female Torso," and "The Offices of Women" appeared as a chapbook called *Scurrilous Toy*, published as part of the 2007 Dusie Kollektiv issue.

Foursquare: "This is a curious machine."

Jumps Journal: "Whence All This Delight"

PennSound: A recording of most of the poems in the "For Girls" section is hosted online at writing.upenn.edu/pennsound/x/Segue_BPC.html. (See October 14, 2006.) Thanks to Nada Gordon and Gary Sullivan, curators of the Segue Series, for arranging this reading.

SOON Productions: "No Slight Affliction, as Many a Woman Will Declare" was published as a broadside designed by Aaron Tieger, for the SOON reading series in November 2006.

The Tiny: "Begins with *F,* Ends with *Uture,*" and "The Dome Is It"

Shanna Compton's books and chapbooks include *Down Spooky,* (Winnow, 2005), *GAMERS: Writers, Artists & Programmers on the Pleasures of Pixels,* (Soft Skull, 2004), *Big Confetti* (with Shafer Hall, Half Empty/Half Full, 2004), *Closest Major Town* (Half Empty/Half Full, 2006), and *Scurrilous Toy* (Dusie Kollektiv, 2007). Her poems and essays have appeared widely in magazines and anthologies, including *The Best American Poetry 2005, The Bedside Guide to No Tell Motel, Exchange Values Vol 2., Bowery Women,* and the Poetry Foundation website. She lives in a valley near a river in New Jersey.

www.shannacompton.com